Cook & Enjoy
for kids

S.J.A. de Villiers and Eunice van der Berg

Learn to cook with
Cook & Enjoy for Kids

This book will show you how easy it is to cook – and what fun it is too.

If you use this book you will be able to make a whole meal for the family, or help your mother by making one of the dishes for a meal. There are also lots of good things to make, just for fun.

Everything you have to do is clearly illustrated, and the methods you will learn are the same as those used in adult cookery books. Once you can make these recipes you will be able to use any cookery book!

**S.J.A. de Villiers
Eunice van der Berg**

contents

Important symbols	**6**
Getting ready	**7**
Facts about foods	**10**
How to measure	**12**
Kitchen equipment	**14**
Place setting	**18**
Words to know	**19**
Drinks	**24**
Breakfast	**32**
Main meals	**44**
Salads, vegetables and rice	**74**
Desserts	**92**
Scones, pancakes and breads	**108**
Biscuits, cakes and sweets	**126**
Who did the cooking?	**160**
Index	**164**

important symbols

These symbols are used in the recipes to make it easy to know what to do.

! The exclamation mark included in some recipes is a reminder to ask a grown-up to help you. Always ask for help when you need to lift any large hot pot or pan, or when you need to take something out of the oven.

This is hot.
Use oven gloves, potholders or oven mittens.

3 SERVINGS The number of people who can eat from the recipe. This is placed next to the recipe name.

 Set the oven temperature to the grade Celsius that is indicated underneath the triangle.

 Grill – put the oven on grill.

6 Cook & Enjoy for Kids

getting ready

1. Ask your mother, or anyone else who can help, to read the recipe with you and show you how to use the kitchen equipment.

2. Wash your hands thoroughly before you start working. Put on an apron to protect your clothes. If you have long hair, tie it back.

3. Set everything out that you need for the recipe before you start working.

remember

1. Use potholders, oven mittens or oven gloves to handle pots, pans and anything hot from the stove so that you do not burn your fingers.

   The ⓘ included in some recipes is a reminder to ask a grown-up to help you. Always ask for help when you need to lift any large hot pot or pan, or when you need to take something out of the oven.

   When lifting the lid of a pot, lift it away from you so that the steam will not burn you. Preferably use a potholder or oven gloves when lifting lids.

2. Turn the handles of saucepans on the stove so that they don't get in your way.

3. Stir hot mixtures with a wooden spoon. A metal spoon might burn your fingers.

4. Be careful when using sharp knives: cut away from you and keep your fingers out of the way.
   Use the correct knife for every recipe. Always cut on a chopping board away from yourself.

5. When grating cheese or vegetables, make sure that your fingers do not touch the grater. When using electric equipment, get a grown-up to help you.

6. Spilt food on the floor might cause an accident. Mop up spills immediately with a damp cloth or paper towel.

afterwards

1. Wash up when you have finished. Utensils used for eggs should first be soaked in cold water. Washing up will then be easier.

2. Put everything you have used back where it belongs. Leave the kitchen tidy when you are finished.

facts about foods

Eating is fun, but you also have to eat certain foods to grow and to keep you healthy. Select some food from each of the following groups every day.

1. **Meat, fish, eggs, milk, cheese, nuts, dried beans and peanut butter**
   This group contains proteins and minerals, which make you grow.

2. **Bread, cereals, noodles and rice**
   This group contains carbohydrates, which provide energy. As wholewheat bread and rusks contain more vitamins and minerals than white bread, they are better sources of energy.

3. **Fruit and vegetables**
   These contain vitamins and minerals that keep you healthy. Make sure that you eat a green vegetable, like green beans, and a yellow vegetable, like carrots, every day. Oranges and guavas contain vitamin C, which helps prevent colds.

4. **Sugar, butter, cream and margarine**
   These add flavour to foods and provide even more energy than bread and cereals. However, you will put on weight if you eat too much of these.

how to measure

Before you start cooking, you must learn to measure ingredients correctly.

Weight is measured in grams (g). A scale is used to do this.
Volume, the contents of a cup or jug, is measured in millilitres (ml). Measuring cups and measuring spoons are used for this purpose.

A set of **measuring spoons** usually includes the following sizes: 15 ml, 10 ml, 7,5 ml, 5 ml, 2 ml and 1 ml. We use these spoons to measure dry ingredients and liquids. If you do not have a set of measuring spoons, use a teaspoon to measure 5 ml and a tablespoon to measure 15 ml.

A set of **measuring cups** is made up of various sizes: 250 ml, 125 ml, 100 ml, 80 ml, 60 ml, 50 ml, 30 ml and 25 ml. There are also sets made up of 1 cup, ¾ cup, ½ cup, ⅓ cup and ¼ cup sizes. They are used to measure dry ingredients.

A **measuring jug** is transparent and the measurements are clearly marked on the side. Use a glass or plastic measuring jug to measure liquids like milk, water or oil. Put the jug on the table and, with your eyes level with the mark on the jug, make sure you have the right amount.

To measure dry ingredients like sugar and flour use the exact size measuring cup required. Spoon the sugar or flour into the clean cup and level off the top with a knife. Do not press the ingredients into the cup.

A **pinch of salt** is the amount of salt you can hold between two fingers.

To measure 75 ml, use a 60 ml measuring cup and a 15 ml measuring spoon.

Butter and margarine are usually sold in 500 g and 250 g blocks. A full 500 g block is equivalent to 500 ml butter or margarine. Cut it through the middle to get two halves of 250 ml each. Cut this through the middle again to measure 125 ml. If you divide one of those, you will have two pieces about 60 ml each.

To measure 15 ml butter or margarine, press butter or margarine firmly into a 15 ml measuring spoon, levelling it off with a knife.

Lengths and widths of pans and baking sheets are measured in centimetres (cm). Use a measuring tape to do this.

To determine the volume of a saucepan or a casserole dish, fill it with cold water. Use a measuring cup to find out how many millilitres it contains.

Cook & Enjoy for Kids

kitchen equipment

Saucepan

Pie dish

Casserole dish

Chopping boards

Muffin pan

Pastry blender

Frying pan

Sharp knife

Baking sheets

Table knife

Vegetable knives

Grater

Bread knife

Wooden, melamine and silicone spoons

Spatula or palette knife

Plastic scrapers

Vegetable peeler

Vegetable brush

Kitchen scissors

Kitchen tongs

Sieve

Potato masher

Colanders

Tin opener

Pastry brushes

Serving spoons

Whisks

Paper towel

Electric hand mixer

Pizza wheel or cutter

Citrus juicer

Garlic press

Egg lifters

Cooling racks

Slotted spoons

Kitchen timers

Food processor

Double boiler or a pot with a heatproof bowl on top

oven temperatures

Oven temperature is regulated by a thermometer in the oven. When an electric oven is switched on, a tiny light goes on. As soon as the desired temperature is reached, the light goes out. You can now place your dish in the oven. Oven thermometers are marked in degrees Celsius (°C) or degrees Fahrenheit (°F). Gauges on gas ovens are marked from 1 to 9.

	Celsius (°C)	Fahrenheit (°F)	Gas
Very cool	100 °C	200 °F	Low
Cool	140 °C	275 °F	Gas 1
Medium cool	160 °C	325 °F	Gas 2
Medium	180 °C	350 °F	Gas 3
Medium hot	190 °C	375 °F	Gas 4
Hot	200–220 °C	400–425 °F	Gas 5–6
Very hot	230–260 °C	450–500 °F	Gas 7–9

place setting

1. Side plate
2. Serviette
3. Butter knife
4. Table fork
5. Plate
6. Table knife
7. Soup spoon
8. Dessertspoon and fork
9. Glass

The cutlery is used starting from the outside to the inside. Cutlery for dessert is set above the plate.

words to know

Bake: to cook in the oven.

Boil: to heat a liquid until air bubbles rise rapidly from the bottom of the pan and break the surface.

Break an egg: to crack the eggshell on the side of a bowl. Place both your thumbs on the crack and break open the egg so that its contents drop into a bowl. Throw away the eggshell.

Chop: to use a sharp knife to cut onions, green peppers, parsley, nuts etc. into small pieces on a chopping board. The pieces should be about the size of a pea. You can also use a food processor to chop ingredients.

Cream: to use the back of a wooden spoon to rub butter or margarine against the sides of a mixing bowl until it looks creamy. Sugar can be added gradually. An electric mixer can also be used.

Cook & Enjoy for Kids 19

Crush: to mash a clove of garlic until fine using a garlic press or the blade of a knife on a chopping board.

Cut in: to blend the butter or margarine with flour using a table knife or pastry blender. The mixture must be fine and look like soft breadcrumbs.

Cut in wedges: to use a sharp knife to cut the fruit or vegetable in half. Cut each half in three or four wedges.

Dissolve: to stir a dry ingredient in a liquid until it disappears, like sugar in water or jelly powder in boiling water.

Drain: to separate liquid from solids. Pour the mixture into a sieve or colander resting on a mixing bowl.

Flake: to use two forks to break an ingredient into small pieces, like boiled fish.

Fold in: to carefully turn the mixture over and over using a metal spoon. The spoon should touch the mixing bowl with every turn. This method of mixing is the best way to retain the air whisked into one of your ingredients like egg whites.

Fry: to cook in oil or butter in a pan.

Grate: to rub cheese or vegetables against the grid of a grater to break it up into regular, fine pieces.

Grease: to spread a little butter or margarine on a baking sheet or oven dish before baking food in it. Use a piece of waxed paper to rub on the butter or margarine. Non-stick cooking spray may be used instead.

Knead: to mix dough by pressing and turning it with your hands until it becomes smooth.

Melt: to heat solids like butter until they form liquids.

Cook & Enjoy for Kids

Mix: to combine different ingredients until they are evenly blended.

Rub in: to blend butter or margarine with flour by rubbing it with your fingertips. Hard (cold) butter or margarine may be grated first. Take care that the heat from your fingers does not melt the butter. Cool your fingers in ice water.

Sauté: to cook food such as onions or mushrooms in a little oil over medium heat without browning.

Separate an egg: to break open the eggshell carefully. Keep the yolk in one half of the shell while the white runs into a bowl. Drop the yolk into another bowl.

Shred: to use a pair of scissors to cut off tiny pieces of an ingredient like herbs. Hold a small bunch of parsley tightly in your left hand while cutting. Take care not to cut your fingers.

Simmer: to cook slowly over a low heat.

 **Slice:** to hold the fruit or vegetable firmly with one hand and use a sharp knife to cut the fruit or vegetable into slices.

 **Stew:** to cook food slowly over low heat in a little water until soft.

 **Stir:** to move a spoon in circles through a mixture in a saucepan or mixing bowl to mix ingredients and to prevent burning. The spoon should touch the bottom of the saucepan.

 **Stir-fry:** to stir chopped or shredded vegetables in a little hot butter or margarine or oil in a frying pan until evenly done. Use a wooden spoon and switch on the stove plate to a medium heat.

 **Whip:** to use a wooden spoon in a rapid up and down movement around the inside of a mixing bowl to get air into a mixture.

 **Whisk:** to use a wire whisk or an electric hand mixer to mix liquids fast or to whisk a lot of tiny air bubbles into a foodstuff like egg whites.

drinks

Banana smoothie	**26**
Chocolate milkshake	**27**
Iced party drink	**28**
Tea for two	**30**

Banana smoothie

1 SERVING

Take out
1 plate
1 fork, 1 mixing bowl
measuring spoons, measuring jug
hand mixer or whisk, 1 large glass
1 saucer, 1 teaspoon

What you'll need
1 ripe banana
5 ml honey
25 ml orange juice
100 ml cold milk
50 ml yoghurt or ice cream

1. Peel the banana and mash it on the plate with the fork. Mix in the honey.

2. Put the banana mixture, orange juice and milk in the mixing bowl. Beat the mixture, using the hand mixer or whisk, until well blended.

3. Beat in the yoghurt or ice cream.

4. Pour the smoothie into the glass and serve on the saucer with a teaspoon.

Chocolate milkshake

1 SERVING

Take out
1 Tupperware® Quick Shake jug
1 soup spoon
measuring spoons, measuring jug
1 large glass

What you'll need
Vanilla or chocolate ice cream
25 ml chocolate syrup
125 ml cold milk

1. Spoon 4 or 5 soup spoons of ice cream into the Quick Shake jug. Add the chocolate syrup and milk. Stir.

2. Put on the lid of the jug and shake well until blended. (You can also use a liquidiser if you have one.)

3. Pour the milkshake into the glass and serve immediately.

drinks

Take out

measuring jug
3 freezer trays for ice cubes
6 glasses
1 vegetable knife
12 coloured straws

What you'll need

375 ml red fruit juice (e.g. red grape, strawberry, raspberry or mixed berry)
375 ml orange or yellow fruit juice (e.g. orange, mango, pineapple or naartjie)
375 ml pale fruit juice (e.g. banana, litchi or white grape)
2 lemons or oranges
750 ml lemonade or soda water

Iced party drink

6 SERVINGS

1. Measure the red, orange and pale fruit juice in turn and pour each into a separate freezer tray.

2. Freeze for at least half a day. Remove from the freezer just before serving.

3. Use the vegetable knife to cut the lemons or oranges into thin slices.

4. Divide the ice cubes between the glasses and then fill the glasses with chilled lemonade or soda water.

5. Place a slice of lemon or orange and two coloured straws in each glass. Serve immediately.

drinks 29

Tea for two

2 SERVINGS

Take out

tray and tray cloth
2 cups, 2 saucers, 2 teaspoons
sugar bowl and sugar spoon
1 small milk jug, tea strainer
1 teapot and tea cosy
hot water jug, electric kettle
measuring spoons
measuring jug

What you'll need

tea leaves or tea bags
500 ml boiling water
milk
sugar

1. Arrange the tray as illustrated. The handles of the cups and teapot point in the same direction. The teaspoons also point in that direction. The milk jug and sugar bowl are full. Don't forget the tea strainer.

2. Half-fill the kettle with cold water and switch on. Switch off when the water starts boiling.

30 Cook & Enjoy for Kids

3. Rinse the teapot with a little boiling water.

4. Measure out 10 ml of tea leaves into the hot teapot or use 2 tea bags. Pour about 500 ml boiling water on the tea leaves or bags.

5. Put the lid on and cover the teapot with the tea cosy.

6. Fill the hot water jug with boiling water and place on the tray next to the teapot.

7. Carry the tray to where the tea will be served.

8. Use the tea strainer to strain the tea into the cups. Offer your guest milk and sugar.

drinks **31**

breakfast

Apple and yoghurt breakfast	**34**
Oats porridge in the microwave oven	**35**
Boiled eggs	**36**
Scrambled eggs and cheese	**38**
French toast	**40**
Toasted cheese	**42**

Apple and yoghurt breakfast

4 SERVINGS

Take out

grater
chopping board
4 cereal bowls
measuring spoons
measuring cups
serving spoon
4 dessertspoons

What you'll need

2–4 apples
4 Weet-Bix® biscuits
100 ml raisins
400 ml plain white yoghurt
20 ml brown sugar or honey
45 ml chopped almonds
   or pecan nuts

1. Wash the apples and grate them coarsely on the chopping board.

2. Divide the grated apple equally into the four cereal bowls. Crumble a Weet-Bix biscuit over the apple in each bowl.

3. Spoon 25 ml raisins and 100 ml yoghurt into each bowl. Sprinkle brown sugar or honey and nuts on top.

4. Serve this balanced breakfast, making sure that there is a spoon next to every bowl.

34 Cook & Enjoy for Kids

Oats porridge
in the microwave oven

1 SERVING

Take out

measuring spoons, measuring jug
deep glass mixing bowl
electric kettle
small whisk or fork
serving spoon
cereal bowl, milk jug
dessertspoon

What you'll need

45 ml oats
1 ml salt
15 ml raisins (if you like them)
150 ml boiling water
30 ml milk
3 ml butter or margarine
5 ml sugar or honey

1. Measure the oats, salt, raisins and boiling water and place in the glass mixing bowl.

2. Mix well with the whisk or fork.

3. Put the mixing bowl in the microwave oven.

4. Microwave on high for 20–30 seconds, until the porridge starts to bubble.

5. Open the door of the microwave oven and mix the porridge with the whisk or fork. If the microwave is large enough you do not need to take the dish out of the microwave to do this.

6. Microwave on low (10–15% power) for 5 minutes.

7. Use oven gloves to remove the mixing bowl from the microwave oven and stir well with the whisk or fork.

8. Spoon the porridge into the cereal bowl and serve with milk, butter or margarine and sugar or honey.

breakfast 35

Take out

small saucepan
safety pin or egg piercer
serving spoon, kitchen timer
tea towel
2 egg cups
2 teaspoons, 2 saucers
2 egg cosies (if you have them)

What you'll need

2 eggs, straight from the refrigerator
salt pot and pepper pot

Cooking times based on egg size

size of eggs	for runny yolk	for firmer yolk	for hard-boiled eggs
large	4 minutes	5 minutes	9 minutes
extra large	5 minutes	6 minutes	10 minutes
jumbo	6 minutes	7 minutes	11 minutes

Boiled eggs

2 SERVINGS

1. Fill the saucepan three-quarters full with water and place on one of the stove plates.

2. Switch the stove plate to high and bring the water to the boil.

3. Holding the egg firmly but carefully, pierce a hole in the round end of each egg.

4. Use the serving spoon to lower the eggs, one at a time, into the boiling water. Reduce the heat of the stove plate to medium.

5. Set the kitchen timer according to the size of the eggs.

6. As soon as the kitchen timer sounds, use the serving spoon to remove the eggs from the water and place them on the tea towel. Use the tea towel to place the eggs in the egg cups.

7. Place the egg cups and teaspoons on the saucers and serve. Don't forget the salt and pepper pots.

The round end of an egg is pierced using an egg piercer or safety pin before boiling the egg. This allows the air to escape slowly and prevents the egg from cracking.

breakfast **37**

Take out

mixing bowl
measuring spoons
measuring cups, measuring jug
whisk, frying pan
egg lifter or fork
grater and chopping board
4 breakfast plates
4 forks, 4 knives

What you'll need

5 eggs
2 ml salt
75 ml milk
50 ml butter or margarine
100 ml grated cheese
parsley sprigs for garnish

Scrambled eggs and cheese

4 SERVINGS

1. Break the eggs into the mixing bowl. Add the salt and milk and whisk until well mixed.

2. Place the frying pan on the stove plate and switch it on to medium heat. Melt the butter or margarine in the frying pan until it bubbles.

3. Pour the egg mixture into the pan and turn the heat to low. Stir slowly using the egg lifter or fork until the mixture thickens.

   NOTE: The mixture will thicken on the bottom of the pan first. Scrape the bottom with the egg lifter using long strokes. Take care that the egg does not boil.

4. Sprinkle the grated cheese over the scrambled egg and dish it onto the four breakfast plates. Decorate each plate with a sprig of parsley.

5. Serve with toast or bread.

breakfast

Take out

4 breakfast plates, mixing bowl
measuring spoons
measuring jug, measuring cups
whisk or fork
shallow dish or cereal bowl
frying pan, egg lifter, potholders
4 knives, 4 forks

What you'll need

3 eggs
60 ml milk
2 ml salt
60 ml butter or margarine
4 slices of brown or white bread
20 ml honey

French toast

4 SERVINGS

1. Put the 4 breakfast plates in the warming oven and switch it on.

2. Break the eggs into the mixing bowl. Add the milk and salt and beat until well mixed. Pour this mixture into the shallow dish.

3. Heat the frying pan over a medium heat. Melt 15 ml butter or margarine in the pan until it starts to bubble.

4. Dip two slices bread, one at a time, into the egg mixture to cover both sides.

5. Use the egg lifter to lift the two slices into the hot frying pan. Turn over carefully when they are light brown underneath and fry again until light brown on the other side.

6. Add another 15 ml butter or margarine to the pan if necessary when turning the slices over. Lift the slices slightly to let the melted butter or margarine run in underneath.

7. Place each slice on a breakfast plate. Keep warm in the warming oven while the other two slices are being fried.

8. Serve the French toast with 5 ml honey drizzled on each slice.

Take out

mixing bowl, whisk
measuring cups
measuring spoons
table knife, baking sheet
oven gloves, egg lifter
3 breakfast plates
3 knives, 3 forks

What you'll need

1 egg
250 ml grated cheddar cheese
15 ml melted butter
   or margarine
pinch of salt
3 slices wholewheat bread

Toasted cheese

3 SERVINGS

1. Break the egg into the mixing bowl and use the whisk to beat the egg.

2. Add the grated cheese, melted butter and salt and mix thoroughly.

3. Use the table knife to divide the mixture into three equal parts.

4. Spread one-third evenly on each slice of bread. Place the slices in the centre of the baking sheet.

5. Switch on the oven grill and put the baking sheet 10 cm below the grill. **GRILL**

6. Leave the oven door open and watch the toast. Remove from the oven using oven gloves as soon as the cheese turns golden brown. Switch off the grill.

7. Use the egg lifter to place the toasted cheese slices on the plates and serve immediately.

breakfast 43

main meals

Hot dogs	46
Hamburgers	48
Macaroni cheese	50
White sauce	53
Chicken à la king	54
Crumbed chicken breasts	56
Chicken casserole	58
Tuna casserole	60
Fish cakes	62
Baked meatballs	66
Savoury mince (Bolognaise sauce)	68
Pizza	70

Take out

saucepan
kitchen tongs
bread knife
table knife
measuring spoons
4 paper serviettes

What you'll need

4 Frankfurters
  or Vienna sausages
4 long, soft bread rolls
butter or margarine
  to spread
4 ml prepared mustard
60 ml tomato sauce

Hot dogs

4 SERVINGS

1. Half-fill the saucepan with hot water. Place it on the stove.

2. Switch on the heat to high, and allow water to boil.

3. ⚠ Put the sausages into the boiling water, using the tongs. Switch off the heat. Leave the sausages in the water for 5 minutes.

4. Cut the rolls partly through lengthwise using the bread knife. Spread butter or margarine on both sides.

5. Spread 1 ml mustard and 10 ml tomato sauce on one side of each roll.

6. Remove the sausages from the water, using the tongs, and place one on each roll.

7. Serve the hot dogs while still hot, wrapped in paper serviettes.

main meals 47

Hamburgers

4 SERVINGS

Take out

kitchen scale
measuring spoons
mixing bowl
fork
chopping board
frying pan
egg lifter
paper towel
5 dinner plates
vegetable knife
bread knife
table knife

What you'll need

400 g mince
15 ml lemon juice
15 ml dried breadcrumbs
5 ml braai spice
5 ml salt
1 ml pepper
30 ml oil
1 large tomato
4 round bread rolls
30 ml butter or
  60 ml mayonnaise
4 lettuce leaves, washed (p. 79)

1. Place the mince, lemon juice, breadcrumbs, spice, salt and pepper in the mixing bowl. Stir with a fork or use clean hands to mix it all together.

2. Divide the mince mixture into four equal portions. Shape each portion into a firm ball and place on the chopping board. Press flat with the palm of your hand until about 10 mm thick.

3. Switch on the stove plate to medium heat and place the frying pan on the stove.

4. Heat the oil in the pan but do not let it get too hot. The oil must not smoke.

5. Use the egg lifter to place each burger patty gently in the pan. Be careful here as the hot oil can splatter. Fry the patties for 5 minutes on one side.

6. Slide the egg lifter under each patty to loosen it and then turn it over carefully, making sure not to splatter the hot oil. Fry the other side for 5 minutes.

7. Carefully lift the patties out of the pan and place on two layers of paper towel on a plate.

8. Cut the tomato into four even slices, using the vegetable knife, and set aside on a plate. Use the bread knife to slice the bread rolls in half and then use the table knife to spread butter or mayonnaise on the rolls. Place a roll on each plate.

9. Place a lettuce leaf and a slice of tomato on the bottom half of the roll, and then top with the cooked burger patty.

10. Place the other half of the roll on top and serve immediately.

main meals

Take out

large saucepan
measuring jug
measuring spoons
measuring cups
slotted spoon
wooden spoon

oven gloves
colander or sieve
2 mixing bowls
baking dish
whisk
table knife

Macaroni cheese

4 SERVINGS

Recipe in two parts

Part 1: Macaroni
What you'll need

2 litres hot water
5 ml salt
500 ml uncooked macaroni pieces
15 ml oil

Part 2: Cheese sauce
What you'll need

margarine or butter for greasing
4 eggs
3 ml salt
2 ml mustard powder
500 ml milk
150–250 ml grated cheddar cheese
15 ml margarine or butter

Part 1

1. Half-fill the saucepan with hot water. Put it on the stove and switch the heat on high. Add salt when the water starts to boil. Reduce the heat to medium.

2. Put the macaroni into the boiling water using the slotted spoon. Boil for 15 minutes. Stir occasionally with the wooden spoon to prevent the macaroni from sticking to the bottom of the saucepan.

3. Remove the saucepan from the stove, using oven gloves. Spoon the macaroni into the colander or sieve which is placed over a mixing bowl.

4. Spoon the oil over the macaroni and stir through.

main meals 51

Part 2

1. Switch on the oven to 160 °C (325 °F).

2. Grease the baking dish with the butter or margarine.

3. Whisk the eggs, salt and mustard powder in the other mixing bowl.

4. Add the milk and stir in the cooked macaroni and the cheese.

5. Pour the mixture into the baking dish and dot with butter or margarine.

6. Bake for 45–60 minutes. Use oven gloves to remove the baking dish from the oven.

7. Insert the table knife into the dish to see if it is done. If the knife comes out clean, the mixture is cooked. If the knife is milky, return the dish to the oven for another 15 minutes.

8. Serve with tomato wedges or tomato sauce, and fresh bread.

White sauce

Take out
glass measuring jug
saucepan
measuring spoons
wooden spoon or whisk

What you'll need
250 ml milk
30 ml butter or margarine
30 ml cake flour
1–2 ml salt

1. Heat the milk in the glass jug for 1 minute on high in the microwave oven.

2. Place the saucepan on the stove and switch on the heat to low.

3. Melt the butter or margarine in the saucepan and stir in the flour and salt. Do not let the flour brown.

4. Add milk gradually while stirring.

5. Continue stirring with the wooden spoon or whisk until the mixture thickens and starts to boil. Switch off the heat.

6. Use the white sauce in chicken à la king **(recipe on p. 55)**, on cauliflower, or as required.

main meals 53

Take out

saucepan
measuring spoons
vegetable knife
chopping board
measuring cups
wooden spoon
measuring jug

What you'll need

30 ml butter or margarine
125 ml chopped onion
125 ml green pepper strips
   (p. 80)
5 ml chicken stock powder
500 ml chopped deboned
   cooked chicken
15 ml chopped parsley
250 ml white sauce
   (recipe on p. 53)
75 ml milk

Chicken à la king

4 SERVINGS

1. Place the saucepan on the stove and switch on the heat to high.

2. Melt the butter or margarine in the saucepan and stir in the chopped onion and green pepper.

3. Stir all the time so that the vegetables do not burn. Reduce the heat to medium after 3 minutes and continue stirring until the vegetables are tender. Sprinkle over the chicken stock powder.

4. Add the chopped chicken and parsley and stir slowly until the chicken is hot.

5. Switch off the heat and leave the mixture in the saucepan while preparing the white sauce **(recipe on p. 53)**.

6. Add the chicken mixture and milk to the hot white sauce as soon as it is ready. Stir slowly to blend until it boils again. Switch off the heat.

7. Serve on toast or boiled rice **(recipe on p. 83)**.

main meals

Crumbed chicken breasts

4 SERVINGS

Take out

measuring cups
measuring spoons
3 soup bowls
whisk
fork
serving platter
large frying pan
egg lifter
paper towel

What you'll need

50 ml cake flour
5 ml salt
2 pinches of pepper
1 ml braai spice
2 ml chicken spice
2 eggs
125 ml dried breadcrumbs
4 chicken breasts, skin removed and deboned
2 x 30 ml oil

1. Mix the flour, salt, pepper and spices together in one of the soup bowls.

2. Beat the eggs in the second soup bowl. Place the breadcrumbs in the third soup bowl.

3. Place the bowls in a row, first the flour, then the eggs and lastly the breadcrumbs.

4. Use the fork to place one chicken breast in the flour and turn until it is completely covered. Dip the chicken breast in the egg, and then in the breadcrumbs.

56 Cook & Enjoy for Kids

5. Do the same with the three remaining chicken breasts, and then place them on the platter and refrigerate until well chilled.

6. Switch on the stove plate to medium heat and place the frying pan on the stove plate. Heat 30 ml of the oil in the pan and spread out using the egg lifter. Do not let the oil overheat and begin to smoke.

7. Using the egg lifter, gently place two of the chicken breasts (one at a time) into the hot pan. Be careful not to let the oil splash out.

8. Fry for 5 minutes on one side, then turn carefully and fry for another 4–5 minutes on the other side until golden brown.

9. Lift the chicken breasts out of the pan and place on a plate lined with two layers of paper towel. Return the pan to the stove plate. Place the chicken onto the serving platter and keep warm in the warming oven.

10. Heat the remaining 30 ml oil in the pan and fry the remaining chicken breasts in the same way as described in steps **7** and **8**.

11. Serve with a tossed green salad **(p. 76)** or vegetables.

Chicken casserole

4-6 SERVINGS

Take out

casserole (1,5 litre)
paper towel, scissors
sharp knife, chopping board
shallow dish, measuring jug
oven gloves, wooden spoon
tablespoon, cup

What you'll need

8 chicken thighs
1 packet dry mushroom soup
375 ml apricot juice
250 g washed fresh or
    tinned mushrooms

1. Set the oven temperature to 160 °C (325 °F).
    160 °C

2. Wash the chicken thighs under cold running water. Dry every piece with paper towel. Trim off any excess fat using the sharp knife and the chopping board or use the scissors.

3. Cut open the packet of soup and empty it into the shallow dish.

4. Roll each thigh in the dry soup mixture and arrange it in the casserole, placing the skin facing upwards.

5. Sprinkle the chicken with remaining soup powder, and pour the apricot juice over, making sure the juice wets all the soup powder.

6. Put on the lid or cover with foil. Place the casserole in the oven for 30 minutes.

7. Using oven gloves, take the casserole out of the oven. Lift the lid carefully so that the steam escapes away from you.

8. Stir in the mushrooms without breaking the chicken thighs. Place the open casserole in the oven for another 20–25 minutes.

9. If necessary, spoon the excess floating fat off the top into the cup, using the tablespoon. Switch off the oven and serve the casserole with boiled rice **(p. 83)**.

main meals **59**

Tuna casserole

4 servings

Take out

- tin opener
- casserole (1 litre)
- whisk
- measuring jug
- mixing bowl
- fork
- plastic bag
- rolling pin
- measuring cups
- oven gloves

What you'll need

- 1 tin cream of chicken soup (405 g)
- 1 egg
- 150 ml milk
- 1 large packet (125 g) potato crisps or 500 ml soft breadcrumbs mixed with 5 ml salt
- 1 tin tuna (200 g)
- 250 ml cooked or tinned green peas

1. Set the oven temperature to 180 °C (350 °F).
   180 °C

2. Open the tin of soup and empty the contents into the casserole.

3. Whisk the egg and milk together in the mixing bowl. Add it to the soup in the casserole. Mix, using a fork.

4. Put the potato crisps in a plastic bag, but do not tie the bag. Crush them with the rolling pin. Add 200 ml crushed crisps or the breadcrumb mixture to the soup mixture.

5. Open the tin of tuna and drain the oil or water. Flake the tuna with a fork and add it to the soup mixture.

6. Lastly, stir in the peas and level the top with the fork. Sprinkle the remaining crushed chips or breadcrumbs on top.

7. Place the casserole in the oven and bake for 30–40 minutes. Use oven gloves to remove the casserole from the oven. Switch off the oven.

8. Serve with a mixed green salad.

main meals

Take out

vegetable brush
vegetable peeler
vegetable knife
chopping board, saucepan
fork, colander, mixing bowls
potato masher
measuring spoons
measuring cups, tin opener
plate, shallow dish
frying pan, egg lifter
paper towel

What you'll need

2 medium potatoes, scrubbed
1 egg, beaten
15 ml chopped parsley
3–4 ml salt
1 ml pepper
150 ml dried breadcrumbs
1 tin pilchards in
    tomato sauce (425 g)
2 x 30 ml oil

Fish cakes

6 SERVINGS

1. Peel the potatoes using the vegetable peeler, and then cut the potatoes into cubes using the vegetable knife and chopping board.

2. Place the potato cubes in the saucepan, add just enough water to cover and then place on the stove plate. Switch on the heat to high and put the lid on the saucepan. Reduce the heat to low as soon as the water comes to the boil and continue to cook until the potatoes are soft.

3. You can check if the potatoes are soft by pricking them with a fork. Add a little water in case there is none left before the potatoes are soft.

4. Drain the water by empting the saucepan into the colander and allow to cool slightly. Place the potatoes in a mixing bowl and mash using the potato masher.

5. Add the egg, parsley, salt and pepper to the mashed potatoes and mix well. Add 75 ml of the dried breadcrumbs and stir until mixed through.

main meals

6. Open the tin of pilchards and empty the contents into the other mixing bowl. Mash with a fork and discard any large visible bones.

7. Add the pilchards to the mashed potato mixture and mix well with a fork.

8. Divide the mixture into six equal portions. Roll each portion into a ball and then flatten slightly. Place on a plate in the refrigerator for about 10 minutes to firm up.

9. Place the rest of the breadcrumbs in the shallow dish and roll each fish cake in the crumbs until well coated.

10. Switch on the stove plate to medium and heat 30 ml oil in the frying pan. Use the egg lifter to gently lower three fish cakes into the pan. Be careful that the oil does not splash out.

11. Fry for 5–8 minutes on one side. Turn over and fry for 5 minutes on the other side until golden brown. Remove the fish cakes from the pan and place on a plate lined with two layers of paper towel. Keep the fish cakes warm in the warming oven.

12. Return the pan to the stove plate and heat the remaining 30 ml oil. Cook the remaining fish cakes in the same way as described in steps **10** and **11**.

13. Serve with tossed green salad **(p. 76)** and oven chips **(p. 90)**.

main meals **65**

Baked meatballs

4 SERVINGS

Take out

serving dish
muffin pan (12 cups)
large mixing bowl
measuring jug
whisk, small mixing bowl
scissors, fork
vegetable knife, chopping board
tablespoon, oven gloves

What you'll need

butter or margarine for greasing
1 Weet-Bix® biscuit
250 ml milk
1 egg
1 packet dry mushroom soup
1 medium tomato
500 g minced beef
1 medium onion, finely chopped

1. Switch on the warming oven and place the serving dish inside. Set the oven temperature at 160 °C (325 °F).

2. Grease the muffin cups with butter or margarine.

3. Put the Weet-Bix in the large mixing bowl and pour the milk over it.

4. Whisk the egg in the small mixing bowl and add to the soaked Weet-Bix.

66 Cook & Enjoy for Kids

5. Cut open the soup packet with the scissors and shake the contents into the Weet-Bix mixture. Mix everything together with a fork.

6. Cut the tomato into small cubes on the chopping board.

7. Stir the mince, chopped tomato and chopped onion into the Weet-Bix mixture and mix well.

8. Spoon the mixture into the muffin cups, round off the tops and bake in the oven for 40 minutes.

9. Take the pan out of the oven using oven gloves. Switch off the oven. Arrange the meatballs in the hot serving dish and serve with baked potatoes **(p. 88)**. They can also be served cold with salad.

main meals **67**

Take out

saucepan
garlic press
vegetable knife
chopping board
grater
wooden spoon, fork
tin opener
measuring spoons
mixing bowl
tablespoon
serving dish

What you'll need

30 ml oil
1 clove garlic, crushed (p. 19)
1 large onion, finely chopped
1 carrot, peeled and grated (p. 21)
400 g mince
1 tin chopped tomatoes (410 g)
10 ml dried basil
30 ml tomato paste
5 ml salt
1 ml pepper

Savoury mince
(Bolognaise sauce)

4 SERVINGS

1. Switch on a stove plate to medium heat. Place the saucepan on the stove plate.

2. Heat the oil in the saucepan and then add the garlic, onion and carrot. Stir-fry for 6 minutes, adding a little water (15–30 ml) if the vegetables start to burn.

3. Add the mince and stir-fry for about 12 minutes over medium heat, stirring often with the wooden spoon so that the mince does not stick to the base of the saucepan. Use the fork to break up any lumps of mince, being careful not to get burned by the steam.

4. Open the tin of tomatoes and stir the contents into the mince mixture. Stir in the basil and tomato paste. Bring the mixture to the boil, and then reduce the heat to low. Simmer for 40 minutes.

5. Stir in the salt and pepper and then spoon the mixture into the serving dish.

6. Serve the savoury mince over macaroni **(p. 51)**, toast or boiled rice **(p. 83)**.

main meals

Take out

saucepan
vegetable knife
chopping board
garlic press
wooden spoon
tin opener
measuring spoons
rolling pin
1 or 2 baking sheets
tablespoon
grater, measuring cups
oven gloves, palette knife
pizza wheel or cutter
  or sharp knife

What you'll need

15 ml butter or margarine
1 onion, chopped (p. 19)
1 clove garlic, crushed (p. 19)
1 tin chopped tomatoes (410 g)
3 ml oregano
2 ml salt
pinch of pepper
250 g white bread dough or
  2 ready-made pizza bases
250 ml grated mozzarella
  cheese
250 ml pineapple pieces
125 ml chopped ham
  or other cold meats

Pizza

Use ready-made dough that your mother can buy at your supermarket's bakery or ask her to make dough for you. You can also use ready-made pizza bases from the supermarket.

Make a tomato sauce:

1. Switch on a stove plate to medium heat. Place the saucepan on the stove plate and melt the butter or margarine in it.

2. Sauté the onion and garlic in the melted butter until soft.

3. Open the tin of tomatoes and empty the contents into the saucepan. Bring the mixture to the boil and then reduce the heat to low. Simmer for 15–20 minutes, partially covered with the lid.

4. Stir in the oregano and continue to cook for another 3–5 minutes. Season with the salt and pepper. Switch off the stove plate.

main meals **71**

Make the pizza bases:

1. Knead the dough on the chopping board until it is smooth and elastic and no longer sticks to your hands. Divide the dough into two equal portions.

2. Sprinkle the clean work surface with a little cake flour and then roll one portion of dough into a ball. Press flat and then roll out with the rolling pin until it resembles a flat pizza round. Sprinkle the work surface and rolling pin with flour to prevent sticking.

3. Sprinkle flour on the baking sheet and place the pizza base on top.

4. Make the second pizza base in the same way as directed in steps **1** to **3**.

Pizza:

1. Set the oven temperature to 220 °C (425 °F).

2. Spoon some tomato sauce onto the pizza bases and spread thinly, leaving the outside rim clear of any sauce. **You can store any leftover tomato sauce in an airtight container in the refrigerator for up to 4 days.**

3. Sprinkle an equal amount of cheese over each pizza base. Divide the pineapple and ham into equal portions and arrange on top of the pizza bases.

4. As soon as the oven reaches the required temperature, place the first pizza in the oven and bake for 10–15 minutes or until the cheese begins to bubble.

5. Open the oven door carefully and step back to allow the steam to escape.

6. Use the oven gloves to remove the baking sheet and place it on a wooden chopping board. Put the second pizza in the oven.

7. Use the palette knife to loosen the pizza from the baking sheet and then slide the pizza onto a large wooden board. Cut into slices with the pizza wheel or cutter or sharp knife.

8. Remove the second pizza from the oven as soon as it is ready and repeat steps **6** and **7**.

main meals

salads, vegetables and rice

Tossed green salad	**76**
Packed crisp salad	**78**
Boiled rice	**83**
Boiled green beans and other vegetables	**84**
Boiled potatoes	**86**
Baked potatoes	**88**
Oven chips	**90**

Tossed green salad

4 SERVINGS

Take out

salad bowl
vegetable knife
chopping board
measuring spoons
salad servers

What you'll need

6 crisp lettuce leaves
½ small cucumber (about 8 cm)
2 tomatoes
4 spring onions
1 ripe avocado
60 ml French salad dressing
2 ml salt

1. Wash and dry the **lettuce leaves** (see p. 79) and break them into small pieces in the salad bowl.

2. Cut the **cucumber** into cubes using the vegetable knife. Sprinkle it over the lettuce.

3. Wash and cut the **tomatoes** into wedges (see p. 20). Arrange them on top of the cucumber.

4. Wash the **spring onions** under cold running water. Pull off the thin outer skin and cut off the roots and some of the green leaves.

5. Cut the spring onions into small rings and sprinkle over the tomato in the salad bowl.

6. Cut the **avocado** lengthwise into two and remove the stone. Peel carefully. Ripe avocado bruises easily, so take care!

7. Dice the avocado and arrange over the other layers.

8. Shake the bottle of **French salad dressing** and pour 60 ml over the salad just before serving.

9. Toss the salad and dressing lightly, using the salad servers. Move the salad around until all the ingredients are evenly coated with the dressing. Season with salt.

salads, vegetables and rice

Take out

large mixing bowl
measuring spoons, measuring jug
tray or serving platter

vegetable peeler
vegetable knife
chopping board

What you'll need

Have a look in the refrigerator and **choose** at least one **green** and one **yellow** vegetable for the salad. Add any of the ingredients from the list below.

6 small carrots
1 sweet pepper (green, red or yellow)
2 tomatoes

1 cucumber
5 ml salt
4–6 crisp lettuce leaves
1 pineapple

Packed crisp salad

4-6 SERVINGS

How to prepare salad ingredients:

1. Wash the **carrots**, **sweet pepper**, **tomatoes** and **cucumber** in cold water in the sink.

2. Empty the sink and rinse the vegetables under cold running water. Do not bruise the vegetables.

3. Dissolve the salt in 1 litre of cold water in the mixing bowl.

4. Wash the **lettuce leaves**, one at a time, in the salt water.

5. Pour out the salt water and rinse the bowl with fresh water. Pour iced water into the mixing bowl and immerse the lettuce leaves for 5 minutes.

6. Shake the water off the lettuce leaves.

7. Tear the lettuce leaves into smaller pieces and arrange in a row on the tray or serving platter.

salads, vegetables and rice **79**

How to peel and cut salad ingredients:

Carrots

1. Peel carrots with a vegetable peeler, using long strokes away from you.

2. Cut off the thick ends with the vegetable knife.

3. Rinse once again and arrange them on the tray or serving platter.

Sweet pepper

1. Cut the pepper into rings on the chopping board.

2. Cut away all the seeds and white ridges on the inside of each ring.

3. Arrange the rings in a row next to the other vegetables on the tray or serving platter.

Cucumber

1. Cut about 12 cm off the cucumber and remove the stem end.

2. Peel thinly with a vegetable peeler, working away from you. (If the cucumber skin is very thin, you do not need to peel it.)

3. Cut the cucumber into thin slices and arrange them in a row on the tray next to the other vegetables.

Tomatoes

1. Cut tomatoes into two halves from top to bottom. Remove the white stem ends.

2. Cut each half into three wedges and arrange them in a row on the tray or serving platter.

salads, vegetables and rice

Pineapple

1. Cut away 2 cm of each end of the pineapple using the vegetable knife on the chopping board.

2. Stand the pineapple on one end and peel in long thin strips from top to bottom.

3. Cut out the eyes with the tip of the vegetable knife or vegetable peeler.

4. Discard the peels and wash the board to remove all thorny bits.

5. Now cut the pineapple into round slices and arrange them in a row on the tray or serving platter. (Cut the round slices in half if the pineapple is very large.)

Boiled rice

6 SERVINGS

Take out

measuring jug, saucepan
measuring spoons
measuring cup, wooden spoon
fork, serving dish

What you'll need

750 ml hot water
5 ml salt
250 ml uncooked rice

1. Pour the hot water into the saucepan. Switch on the stove plate to a medium heat. Allow the water to boil.

2. Add the salt and rice. Stir with a wooden spoon. Leave to boil and do not stir any longer. Reduce the heat to low.

3. Cover the saucepan and leave to simmer for 40 minutes until cooked.

4. The rice grains will be swollen and there should be no water left at the bottom. Small holes will have formed in the rice. Switch off the heat.

5. Loosen the rice with the fork and spoon it into the serving dish.

salads, vegetables and rice

Take out

vegetable knife, chopping board
measuring cups, saucepan
fork, measuring spoons
serving dish

What you'll need

500 g green beans
250 ml hot water
2 ml salt
5–10 ml butter or margarine

Other vegetables can be cooked in the same way. Adjust the cooking time as follows:

Vegetable	Cooking time
carrots, peeled (p. 80) and sliced	15–20 minutes
baby marrows, washed and sliced	6–10 minutes
cauliflower and broccoli, washed and broken into pieces	4–6 minutes
frozen peas (you need only 125 ml water for cooking)	2–4 minutes (on high)
cabbage, sliced or chopped	4–6 minutes
gem squash, cut in half and pips taken out with a teaspoon	20 minutes

Boiled green beans
and other vegetables

1. Wash the beans in cold running water.

2. Cut off the stems with the vegetable knife. Slice the beans. Young green beans may be cooked whole (you only need to cook these for 6 minutes).

3. Pour the hot water into the saucepan. Switch on the stove plate to high and allow the water to boil.

4. Add the beans to the boiling water. Put on the lid of the saucepan. Reduce the heat to medium once the water boils again.

5. Cook the beans for 10 minutes. Prick the beans with a fork to test for tenderness. Add a little extra water in case the beans are still too firm and the saucepan has already boiled dry.

6. Add the salt. Switch off the heat. Drain the water.

7. Serve the beans in the serving dish and dot with butter or margarine.

salads, vegetables and rice **85**

Take out

vegetable brush, vegetable knife
chopping board, saucepan
measuring spoons
slotted spoon, serving dish

What you'll need

4 medium potatoes
3 ml salt
butter or margarine

Boiled potatoes

4 SERVINGS

1. Scrub the potatoes with the vegetable brush under running water to remove all the soil and dirt.

2. Cut each potato through lengthwise on the chopping board.

3. Put the potatoes in the saucepan with the rounded skin-side facing down. Cover the potatoes with hot water and put the lid on the saucepan.

4. Put the saucepan on the stove over a high heat. When the water starts boiling, reduce the heat to medium.

5. Boil the potatoes for 25–30 minutes. Add a little extra water if necessary.

6. Sprinkle the salt over the potato halves in the saucepan. Spoon them out with a slotted spoon and place in the serving dish.

7. Dot each potato half with butter or margarine before serving.

salads, vegetables and rice

Take out
vegetable brush
fork, baking sheet
oven gloves
dinner plate
clean dishcloth, knife

What you'll need
4 medium potatoes
butter or margarine

Baked potatoes

4 SERVINGS

1. Set the oven temperature to 200 °C (400 °F).

2. Scrub the potatoes with the vegetable brush under running water. Remove all the soil and dirt. **(See point 1 p. 87)**.

3. Prick each potato once with a fork to prevent its skin bursting in the oven.

4. Place the potatoes on the baking sheet. Place the baking sheet on an oven rack in the middle of the oven. Leave to bake for 35–45 minutes. Switch off the oven.

5. Take the baking sheet from the oven using oven gloves. Place the potatoes on the dinner plate. They will feel soft if they are ready.

6. Roll the potatoes, one at a time, in the dishcloth. This will loosen the skin and soften them slightly.

7. Cut a cross through the skin of each potato using the dishcloth to hold it. Squeeze each potato slightly to open at the cross until the white shows.

8. Serve with a pat of butter on the cross of each potato.

salads, vegetables and rice **89**

Oven chips

4 SERVINGS

Take out

vegetable brush, vegetable knife
chopping board, paper towel
large plastic freezer bag
baking sheet, tin foil
oven gloves, fork, serving dish

What you'll need

8 medium potatoes
   or sweet potatoes
45 ml oil
salt

1. Set the oven temperature to 200 °C (400 °F).
   200 °C

2. Scrub the potatoes **(see p. 87)** with the vegetable brush under running water. Remove all the soil and dirt. Dry thoroughly.

3. Cut the potatoes in half lengthwise. Cut each half again lengthwise in three. Each wedge must have some peel on it.

90 Cook & Enjoy for Kids

4. Dry the wedges, one at a time, with paper towel and place them in the freezer bag.

5. Pour the oil into the freezer bag.

6. Tie the bag and shake until all the wedges are coated with the oil.

7. Cover the baking sheet with a layer of tin foil. Empty the potato wedges onto the foil and arrange them so that the peel side is underneath.

8. Place the baking sheet on a rack in the middle of the oven and bake for 30 minutes or until the chips start to brown.

9. Remove the baking sheet from the oven using oven gloves and test the chips with a fork to make sure they are soft.

10. Sprinkle the salt over the chips and serve immediately in the serving dish.

salads, vegetables and rice

desserts

Trifle 94

Jelly 97

Custard 98

Orange pudding 100

Baked sago pudding 104

Apple Brown Betty 106

Trifle

Take out

table knife
chopping board
measuring spoons
pudding bowl
measuring jug
spoon
measuring cups
fork
whisk
small mixing bowl

What you'll need

6 slices sponge cake or swiss roll
40 ml smooth apricot jam
100 ml apricot juice or 100 ml orange juice
90 ml chopped pecan nuts
50 ml chopped green fig preserve (if you like it)
450 ml custard (p. 98)
red jelly (prepare beforehand, using 125 ml cold water instead of 250 ml, see p. 97)
125 ml cream

1. Spread the sponge cake slices with apricot jam. Cut into pieces.

2. Arrange the pieces in the pudding bowl.

3. Sprinkle the cake with the apricot juice or orange juice using the spoon. Sprinkle the nuts and green fig preserve on top.

desserts 95

4. Pour the custard evenly over the damp sponge cake and leave for 30 minutes.

5. Use a fork to break up the firm jelly in the bowl in which it has set.

6. Spoon the red jelly on top of the custard in the pudding bowl.

7. Use the whisk to whip the cream in the small mixing bowl, taking care not to whip for too long. The whipped cream should be just firm enough to stick to the whisk.

8. Spoon some of the whipped cream in the middle of the trifle on top of the custard. Serve the rest of the cream with the trifle.

Jelly

Take out

scissors, mixing bowl
measuring jug, wooden spoon
1 pudding bowl or
 4 individual pudding glasses

What you'll need

1 packet jelly
250 ml boiling water
250 ml cold water

1. Cut open the jelly packet with the scissors and shake the contents into the mixing bowl.

2. Pour the boiling water over and stir with the wooden spoon to dissolve all the jelly crystals. Make sure that there are no crystals stuck to the wooden spoon or mixing bowl.

3. Stir in the cold water.

4. Pour the jelly into the pudding bowl or glasses and leave it in the refrigerator to set.

desserts 97

Custard
(450 ml)

4 SERVINGS

Take out

2 mixing bowls
measuring spoons
measuring jug
wooden spoon, whisk
plate, saucepan
milk jug (500 ml)

What you'll need

30 ml custard powder
15–30 ml sugar
pinch of salt
50 ml cold milk
1 egg, 2 ml vanilla essence
400 ml hot milk

1. Blend the custard powder, sugar and salt in one mixing bowl. Stir in 50 ml cold milk with the wooden spoon until smooth.

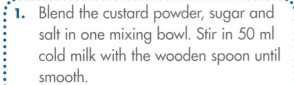

2. Whisk the egg in the other mixing bowl for 1 minute. Rest the whisk on the plate until needed again.

3. Switch on the stove plate to a medium heat. Boil the milk in the saucepan. Reduce the heat to low as soon as the milk starts boiling.

4. Pour a little hot milk into the custard powder mixture and stir well.

98   Cook & Enjoy for Kids

5. Replace the saucepan with remaining milk on the stove. Add the custard powder mixture, stirring all the time with the wooden spoon.

6. Stir the custard continuously until it thickens and boils again. Let it boil slowly for 3 minutes. Continue stirring.

7. Remove the saucepan from the heat and call someone to help you.

8. Beat the egg again with the whisk while the other person pours the boiling mixture slowly onto the egg.

9. Add the vanilla essence and whisk again to blend.

10. Pour the custard back into the saucepan and stir it over a low heat until it starts to boil again. Keep stirring.

11. Switch off the stove plate and remove the saucepan. Stir the custard for a while after you have removed it from the stove.

12. Allow the custard to cool. Pour it into the jug.

desserts 99

Take out

grater, small plate, fork
vegetable knife, citrus juicer
measuring jug
measuring cups, tea cup
measuring spoons, teaspoon
small mixing bowl
large mixing bowl
electric hand mixer, tablespoon
pudding dish (1,5 litre)

What you'll need

1 orange
500 ml orange juice (fresh or store-bought)
60 ml cold water
25 ml gelatine
60 ml boiling water
3 eggs, separated (p. 19)
200 ml sugar

Orange pudding

6 SERVINGS

1. Wash the orange in cold water and wipe dry.

2. Grate the outer yellow rind of the orange on the finest grid of the grater. Remove the grated rind from the grater with the fork. You should have about 5 ml yellow rind. It will look like an oily pulp.

3. Cut the orange in half with the vegetable knife and squeeze out the orange juice with the citrus juicer. Pour the juice into the measuring jug. Add more orange juice until you have 500 ml.

4. Measure out 60 ml cold water into the tea cup. Sprinkle the gelatine powder on the cold water so that all of it gets wet. Leave for 5 minutes until it thickens.

desserts

5. Pour the 60 ml boiling water on the gelatine and stir it with a teaspoon. It will become clear when the gelatine has dissolved.

6. Separate the eggs carefully. Drop the egg whites into the small mixing bowl and the yolks into the large mixing bowl.

7. Whisk the egg yolks with the electric hand mixer. Whisk in the sugar one spoonful at a time. The mixture will become creamy and light.

8. Add the orange rind and orange juice. Stir with the tablespoon. Add the gelatine and stir until well mixed.

9. Leave the mixture in the fridge until it starts to set. Draw a spoon through the pudding to make sure that it is partly set.

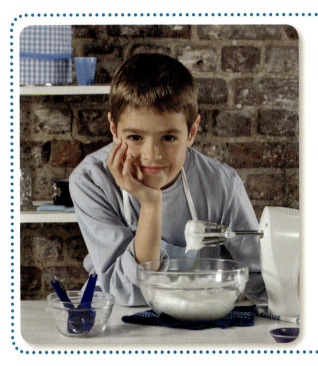

10. Wash the whisk and dry it thoroughly. Whisk the egg whites until a stiff white foam clings to the whisk. Do not whisk any longer. Whisk the partly set pudding with the same whisk (you do not need to wash it first).

11. Fold the stiff egg whites carefully into the thick orange pudding using the tablespoon (see p. 21). Do not stir.

12. Pour the orange dessert into the pudding bowl and allow it to set properly in the fridge. Serve it with cream or custard (p. 98).

Baked sago pudding

6 SERVINGS

Take out

measuring jug
measuring cups, saucepan
wooden spoon, whisk
mixing bowl
measuring spoons
baking dish (1 litre)
oven pan, water jug
oven gloves

What you'll need

400 ml milk
50 ml sago
butter or margarine for greasing
2 eggs
20–40 ml sugar
1 ml salt
5 ml vanilla essence

1. Measure out 100 ml milk into the measuring jug. Soak the sago in it for 1 hour.

2. Set the oven temperature to 150 °C (300 °F). Grease the baking dish with butter or margarine. 150 °C

3. Switch on a stove plate to medium heat and bring the remaining 300 ml milk to the boil in the saucepan. Reduce the heat to low.

4. Stir the soaked sago into the hot milk with the wooden spoon. Let it boil for 5 minutes while stirring all the time. Switch off the heat.

Cook & Enjoy for Kids

5. Beat the eggs, sugar, salt and vanilla essence with the whisk in the mixing bowl.

6. Add the hot sago mixture to the beaten egg and sugar.

7. Pour the mixture into the greased baking dish. Place the dish in the centre of the oven pan.

8. Fill the water jug with hot water. Pour the water into the oven pan to a depth of 2 cm.

9. Ask a grown-up to place the oven pan on the middle rack in the oven.

10. Bake for 45 minutes. Ask a grown-up to help you remove the pudding from the oven. Switch off the oven.

11. Serve the sago pudding in pudding bowls with syrup or jam.

desserts 105

Apple Brown Betty

4 SERVINGS

Take out

baking dish (1,5 litre)
chopping board, vegetable knife
vegetable peeler
measuring spoons
measuring cups
small saucepan
fork
oven gloves

What you'll need

6 apples
60 ml sugar
100 ml butter or margarine
400 ml soft breadcrumbs
2 ml ground cinnamon
30 ml hot water
15 ml lemon juice

1. Set the oven temperature to 180 °C (350 °F). Grease the baking dish with butter or margarine. 180 °C

2. Quarter the apples on the chopping board with the vegetable knife. Remove the cores and peel them thinly.

3. Cut each quarter into thin slices. Arrange these in the greased baking dish.

106 Cook & Enjoy for Kids

4. Sprinkle 20 ml sugar on the apple slices.

5. Switch on the stove plate to a low heat. Melt the butter or margarine in the saucepan. Remove from the stove.

6. Add the breadcrumbs, the remaining sugar and the cinnamon to the butter. Blend well with the fork.

7. Spread the crumb mixture over the apples and level it with the fork.

8. Mix the hot water and lemon juice and pour it evenly over the crumbs.

9. Bake it in the oven for 30–45 minutes. Remove the dish from the oven using oven gloves. Switch off the oven.

10. Serve with custard (**p. 98**) or cream.

If there is one available, soft breadcrumbs can be prepared in a liquidiser or food processor in a second. Ask someone to help you.

desserts **107**

scones, pancakes and breads

Breakfast scones	110
Cheese scones	114
Bran muffins	116
Crumpets	118
Pancakes	120
Dainty sandwiches	124

Take out

baking sheet, chopping board
measuring cups
measuring spoons
sieve, mixing bowl
pastry blender, measuring jug
whisk, small mixing bowl
table knife, cookie cutter
palette knife (spatula)
pastry brush, oven gloves
cooling rack

What you'll need

15 ml cake flour
500 ml cake flour
20 ml baking powder
3 ml salt
60 ml chilled butter (cut into small cubes)
1 egg
150 ml ice-cold water
15 ml milk
pinch of salt

Breakfast scones

1. Grease the baking sheet with butter and sift 5 ml of the 15 ml cake flour over the whole surface. Sprinkle 10 ml flour on the chopping board.

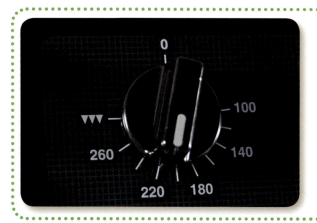

2. Set the oven temperature to 220 °C (425 °F). This is a very hot oven.

3. Sift the 500 ml cake flour, baking powder and salt into the mixing bowl.

4. Rub the butter into the flour with your fingertips or cut it into the flour (p. 25) with the pastry blender until it forms crumbs.

5. Use the whisk to beat the egg and ice-cold water in the small mixing bowl.

scones, pancakes and breads

6. Pour almost all the egg mixture over the flour mixture. Set the small mixing bowl aside.

7. Immediately cut the liquid egg mixture into the flour mixture with the table knife until it is just wet through. Do not mix for any longer.

8. Turn out the dough onto the chopping board. Press it lightly together with your fingers.

9. Rub the dough from your hands into the empty mixing bowl.

10. Lightly press the dough on the board to a thickness of 2 cm. Sprinkle more flour on the board if necessary.

11. Use the cookie cutter to cut round scones out of the dough. Press evenly on the cookie cutter when pushing it through the dough.

12. Cut out all the scones closely together.

13. Lift them carefully onto the baking sheet with the palette knife. Take care not to spoil their shape. Place them 3 cm apart. Press the remaining dough lightly together and cut out more scones.

14. Mix the 15 ml milk and a pinch of salt in the small mixing bowl with the leftover beaten egg. Use the pastry brush to brush some of this mixture over the top of every scone.

15. Bake for 10–12 minutes in the oven. Remove the baking sheet from the oven with oven gloves and put it on the cooling rack. Switch off the oven.

16. Serve the scones hot, with butter and jam.

scones, pancakes and breads

Take out

muffin pan with small cups
   (2,5 cm in diameter)
measuring cups
measuring spoons, sieve
large mixing bowl
pastry blender, measuring jug
whisk, small mixing bowl
table knife, 3 teaspoons
oven gloves

What you'll need

250 ml cake flour
10 ml baking powder
40 ml butter or margarine
1 egg
100 ml milk
150 ml grated cheddar cheese

Cheese scones

1. Set the oven temperature to 190 °C (375 °F). Grease the muffin cups with butter or margarine.

2. Sift the flour and baking powder into the large mixing bowl.

3. Rub the butter or margarine into the flour with your fingertips. It can also be cut with the pastry blender until it looks like breadcrumbs.

4. Use the whisk to beat the egg and milk together in the small mixing bowl.

5. Pour the egg mixture onto the flour mixture.

6. Cut it into the flour mixture in all directions with the table knife. Do not continue mixing after all the flour is wet.

7. Spread the grated cheese over the mixture and mix it in with the knife. Take care not to mix longer than necessary.

8. Use two teaspoons to drop a little dough into every muffin cup.

9. Bake the scones for 10 minutes. Remove the muffin tray from the oven with oven gloves. Switch off the oven.

10. Lift out the scones with a clean teaspoon. Serve while they are still hot.

scones, pancakes and breads

Bran muffins

Take out

muffin pan
measuring cups
measuring spoons, sieve
large mixing bowl
wooden or silicone spoon, whisk
small mixing bowl
tablespoon, oven gloves
cooling rack, palette knife

What you'll need

250 ml cake flour
5 ml bicarbonate of soda
5 ml salt
375 ml bran
1 egg
30 ml oil
250 ml milk
125 ml golden syrup

1. Set the oven temperature to 190 °C (375 °F). Grease the muffin cups with butter or margarine.

2. Sift the flour, bicarbonate of soda and salt into the large mixing bowl. Stir in the bran.

3. Whisk the egg, oil and milk together in the small mixing bowl.

116   Cook & Enjoy for Kids

4. Dip the tablespoon in a cup of boiling water. Use the hot tablespoon to measure 125 ml syrup into the measuring cup that was used for the milk.

5. Add the egg mixture to the syrup. Stir thoroughly with the tablespoon.

6. Add this to the dry mixture and stir at once, just enough to mix.

7. Spoon the mixture into the muffin cups.

8. Bake for 25 minutes. Remove the muffin pan from the oven with oven gloves. Place it on the cooling rack. Switch off the oven.

9. Lift the muffins from the cups with the palette knife. You can put them into a basket lined with a serviette.

10. Serve the muffins hot with butter or margarine and honey.

scones, pancakes and breads 117

Crumpets

Take out

whisk, 2 mixing bowls
measuring cups
measuring jug
measuring spoons
sieve, wooden spoon
serving dish
large frying pan
tablespoon
palette knife (spatula)

What you'll need

1 egg
60 ml castor sugar
150 ml milk
15 ml oil
250 ml cake flour
10 ml baking powder
1 ml salt
butter or margarine
honey

1. Use a whisk to beat the egg in a mixing bowl. Add the castor sugar and beat well.

2. Add half the milk and all the oil to the egg mixture. Beat thoroughly.

118 Cook & Enjoy for Kids

3. Sift the flour, baking powder and salt together in the other mixing bowl.

4. Add the flour mixture gradually to the egg mixture. Stir with a wooden spoon until it is smooth.

5. Stir in the remaining milk slowly until it has blended well. Do not overmix.

6. Switch on the stove plate to medium heat. Put the serving dish in the warming oven and switch on.

7. Grease the frying pan with oil and heat it on the stove plate.

8. Carefully drop 3 or 4 tablespoonfuls of the batter into the hot frying pan. Let each crumpet spread in the pan before the next one is dropped next to it. The crumpets should not touch.

9. Turn the crumpets carefully with the palette knife as soon as bubbles appear on their surfaces.

10. Cook them until they are risen and light brown on both sides. Lift them onto the serving dish.

11. Keep the crumpets warm in the warming oven. Repeat the process until all the batter has been used.

12. Serve the crumpets with butter or margarine and honey.

Take out

measuring cups
measuring spoons, sieve
2 mixing bowls, measuring jug
whisk, tablespoon
saucepan and a dinner plate
  that will fit on top
frying pan or pancake pan
  (20 cm in diameter)
soup ladle
egg lifter or palette knife
  (spatula)
fork

What you'll need

250 ml cake flour
2 ml baking powder
2 large eggs
175 ml milk
175 ml water
1 ml salt
15 ml oil
cinnamon sugar
oil to grease pan

Pancakes

1. Sift the flour and baking powder into a mixing bowl.

2. Beat the eggs, milk, water, salt and 15 ml oil well with the whisk in the other mixing bowl.

3. Add the flour, 3 tablespoons at a time, to the egg mixture. Beat until no lumps are left before the next 3 tablespoons are added. The batter should be thin so that it will spread easily in the hot pan. This will ensure thin pancakes.

4. Half-fill the saucepan with hot water. Put the dinner plate on top. Place the saucepan on one of the back stove plates on medium heat.

5. Switch on stove plate to medium-high. Measure out 2 ml oil into the frying pan and place it on the heat.

6. Tip the pan to spread the oil. Do not heat too long, otherwise the oil might start smoking.

7. Use the 60 ml measuring cup or soup ladle and almost fill it with batter. Let the excess batter drip off into the mixing bowl.

scones, pancakes and breads

8. Hold the hot frying pan with your one hand and empty the measuring cup full of batter in the middle of the pan using your other hand.

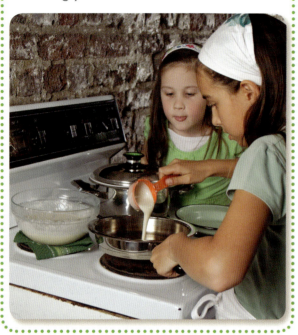

9. Tip the pan so that the batter covers the bottom of the pan.

10. Put the pan back on the heat. As soon as the edges of the pancake become dry and crisp, it is ready to be turned.

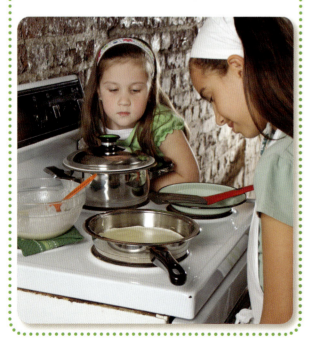

11. Lift the pancake carefully with the egg lifter and turn it over. Fry the other side for about 1 minute.

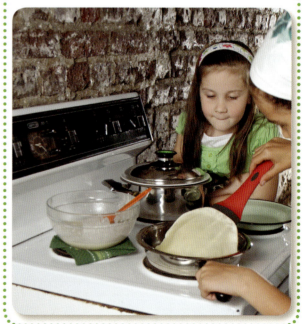

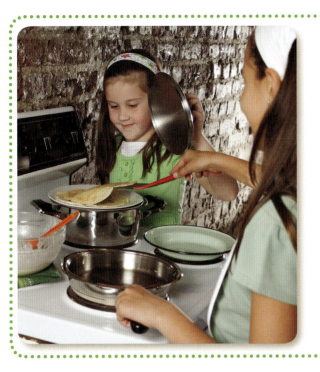

12. Lift the pancake from the pan and place it on the dinner plate over hot water to keep it warm. (The lid of the saucepan can be used to cover the pancakes on the plate.)

13. Cook the other pancakes in the same way steps **10 – 12** until all the batter has been used.

14. Sprinkle cinnamon sugar over each pancake and roll it with a fork before serving it.

Remember that not all stoves have the same high setting. If the pancakes darken too quickly, lower the heat to medium.

scones, pancakes and breads

Take out

plastic bag
rolling pin
bread knife
chopping board
table knife
serving plate

What you'll need

1 small packet (30 g) flavoured potato crisps
4 slices of bread
20 ml soft butter or margarine
50 ml cheese spread or cream cheese, any flavour

Dainty sandwiches

1. Put the potato crisps in the plastic bag. Fold the bag to close and crush the crisps with the rolling pin.

2. Cut off the bread crusts with the bread knife so that the slices match perfectly.

3. Spread one side of each slice with soft butter or margarine. Spread cheese spread or cream cheese on two of the four slices. Place the other two slices on top.

4. Spread butter or margarine over the top of each sandwich.

5. Cut each sandwich into 6 pieces with the bread knife.

6. Sprinkle the crushed potato crisps on top of the butter on each sandwich.

7. Arrange the sandwiches on the serving plate and serve with tea **(p. 30)** or milk.

scones, pancakes and breads **125**

biscuits, cakes and sweets

Date surprises	128	**Party cake (butter cake)**	146
Oats and raisin cookies	130	**Honey cake**	148
Peanut butter biscuits	132	**Peanut clusters**	151
Crisp custard squares	134	**Chocolate clusters**	152
Fairy cakes (cupcakes)	136	**Coconut fudge**	154
Orange biscuits	140	**Crispies**	156
Sugar biscuits	142	**Nut caramels**	158
Butter icing	145		

Take out

vegetable knife
chopping board
saucepan, measuring cups
measuring spoons
whisk, 2 small mixing bowls
wooden spoon
shallow dish

What you'll need

250 g pitted dates
125 g butter or margarine
1 egg
60 ml sugar
20 Marie biscuits
100 ml desiccated coconut

Date surprises

1. Use the vegetable knife to cut up the dates on the chopping board.

2. Switch on the stove plate to low. Melt the butter or margarine in the saucepan on the stove plate.

3. Add the date pieces to the butter or margarine. Stir until the mixture is soft.

4. Whisk the egg and sugar together in one mixing bowl. Stir the egg mixture into the date mixture. Blend thoroughly.

5. Take the saucepan off the stove and place it on the chopping board. Switch off the heat.

6. Use your hands and break the Marie biscuits in small pieces into the other mixing bowl. Stir the pieces into the date mixture. Leave it to cool.

7. Put the coconut into the shallow dish. Roll the date mixture into balls in your hands. Roll each ball in coconut.

8. Arrange the date surprises in a bowl to cool completely until they are firm.

biscuits, cakes and sweets

Take out

2 baking sheets
measuring cups
measuring spoons
sieve
mixing bowl
wooden spoon
2 teaspoons
oven gloves
chopping board
cooling rack
palette knife (spatula)

What you'll need

250 ml cake flour
2 ml salt
2 ml bicarbonate of soda
5 ml ground cinnamon
125 ml soft butter or margarine
125 ml brown sugar
60 ml white sugar
1 egg
25 ml lukewarm milk
150 ml seedless raisins
500 ml oats

Oats and raisin cookies

1. Set the oven temperature to 190 °C (375 °F) Grease the baking sheets with butter or margarine.

2. Sift the flour, salt, bicarbonate of soda and cinnamon together into the mixing bowl.

3. Add the butter or margarine, sugar, egg and milk and stir with a wooden spoon. Beat until the mixture is smooth and well blended. You can use a food processor if one is available.

4. Add the raisins and oats and blend well.

5. Use the two teaspoons to form lumps of dough and place 5 cm apart on the baking sheets.

6. Put one baking sheet at a time in the oven for 12–15 minutes. Use oven gloves to take the baking sheets from the oven. Place them on the chopping board. Lift the cookies onto the cooling rack with the palette knife. Switch off the oven.

biscuits, cakes and sweets

Peanut butter biscuits

Take out

2 baking sheets, measuring cups
2 mixing bowls
wooden spoon or
   electric hand mixer
tablespoon, measuring spoons
sieve, fork, oven gloves
chopping board
palette knife (spatula), cooling rack

What you'll need

125 ml butter or margarine
125 ml peanut butter
125 ml white sugar
125 ml brown sugar
1 egg
325 ml cake flour
1 ml salt
2 ml bicarbonate of soda

1. Set the oven temperature to 180 °C (350 °F). Grease the baking sheets. 180 °C

2. Cream the butter and peanut butter in a mixing bowl using the wooden spoon or electric hand mixer.

3. Add the white and brown sugar two spoonfuls at a time. Beat well after each addition.

132 Cook & Enjoy for Kids

4. When all the sugar has been added, beat in the egg. Do not beat after the mixture is well blended.

5. Sift the flour, salt and bicarbonate of soda together in the other mixing bowl.

6. Stir this mixture gradually into the egg mixture.

7. Knead the dough in the mixing bowl until it is smooth and forms a ball.

8. Roll small round balls of dough in your hands – 10 ml dough is enough for each ball.

9. Place the balls about 5 cm apart in rows on the baking sheets. Flatten each ball with the fork.

10. Bake each baking sheet separately for 15–20 minutes at a time until the biscuits are light brown.

11. Use oven gloves to take the baking sheets from the oven and place them on a chopping board. Switch off the oven.

12. Use the palette knife to place the biscuits on the cooling rack to cool.

Crisp custard squares

20 SQUARES

Take out

flat baking dish or pan
  (20 cm x 16 cm)
measuring cups, mixing bowl
measuring spoons
wooden spoon
palette knife (spatula), fork
oven gloves, chopping board
table knife, serving dish

What you'll need

125 g soft butter or margarine
100 ml icing sugar
50 ml custard powder
1 ml vanilla essence
250 ml cake flour

1. Set the oven temperature to 180 °C (350 °F). Grease the baking dish or pan with butter or margarine.

2. Measure out the butter or margarine into the mixing bowl.

3. Add the icing sugar and custard powder to the butter. Mix thoroughly and add the vanilla essence as well.

4. Add the flour and knead the mixture with your hands until it forms one smooth lump.

5. Press the dough into the baking dish or pan. Smooth the top with the palette knife.

6. Prick the dough lightly with the fork.

7. Put the baking dish in the oven for 20 minutes. Use oven gloves to take it from the oven and place it on the chopping board. Switch off the oven.

8. Cut it into 20 squares with the table knife. Leave them to cool.

9. Use the palette knife to lift the cookies from the pan into a serving dish.

biscuits, cakes and sweets **135**

Fairy cakes
(cupcakes)

Take out

12 paper baking cups
muffin pan, measuring cups
2 mixing bowls
wooden spoon or
 electric hand mixer
tablespoon
measuring spoons
sieve, measuring jug
oven gloves
chopping board
cooling rack
table knife
teaspoon

What you'll need

90 g soft butter or margarine
185 ml castor sugar
5 ml vanilla essence
2 eggs, at room temperature
375 ml cake flour
10 ml baking powder
2 ml salt
100 ml milk
raspberry jam

1. Set the oven temperature to 180 °C (350 °F).

2. Place the paper baking cups in the muffin pan.

3. Cream the butter or margarine in a mixing bowl with the wooden spoon or electric hand mixer.

biscuits, cakes and sweets **137**

4. Add 3 tablespoons castor sugar at a time and beat thoroughly each time until all the sugar has been used. The mixture must be light and creamy.

5. Add the vanilla essence. Add the eggs to the butter mixture and beat again to mix well.

6. Sift the flour, baking powder and salt together in the other mixing bowl.

7. Fold half the flour mixture into the butter mixture with a wooden or tablespoon. Stir in the milk.

8. Fold in the rest of the flour mixture carefully until the batter is well blended. It should be a smooth, thick batter.

9. Spoon equal amounts of batter into the paper cups, using the tablespoon. Take care not to mess bits of the batter around the edges.

10. Place the muffin pan in the oven for 15 minutes or until cooked (a testing skewer must come out clean when inserted into the centre of the cupcakes). Remove the pan from the oven with oven gloves and place it on the chopping board. Turn off the oven heat.

11. Lift the cakes onto the cooling rack to cool.

12. Cut a slice off the top of each little cake with the table knife. Cut the slice in two halves.

13. Put a teaspoon of jam on each little cake. Place the two half slices on top of the jam like butterfly wings.

The fairy cakes can also be decorated with butter icing (p. 145) and colourful sweets.

biscuits, cakes and sweets **139**

Orange biscuits

Take out

2 baking sheets
mixing bowl
wooden spoon or electric hand mixer
tablespoon, measuring spoons
grater, fork, measuring cups
teaspoon, oven gloves
chopping board
palette knife (spatula) or egg lifter
cooling rack

What you'll need

250 g soft butter or margarine
125 ml castor sugar
1 egg
1 orange
750 ml cake flour

Before you start

Remove the butter or margarine from the refrigerator at least 1 hour before starting.

1. Set the oven temperature to 180 °C (350 °F).

2. Grease the baking sheets with butter or margarine.

3. Cream the butter or margarine in the mixing bowl with the wooden spoon or electric hand mixer.

4. Add 3 tablespoons of castor sugar at a time to the butter and beat thoroughly each time until all the sugar has been used.

5. Add the egg to the butter mixture. Beat it just enough to mix well. If the mixture separates, 25 ml of the flour may be added.

6. Grate the yellow rind of the orange on a fine grater. Scrape off all the yellow rind from the grater with a fork **(see illustration no. 2 on p. 101)**. Add it to the butter mixture.

7. Add the flour gradually, mixing with the wooden spoon or electric hand mixer.

8. Knead the dough in the mixing bowl to a fine smooth lump.

9. Break off bits of the dough with a teaspoon. Roll them into balls in your hands.

10. Place the balls 5 cm apart on the baking sheets. Flatten them slightly with a teaspoon.

11. Bake one baking sheet at a time for 20 minutes. Remove it from the oven with oven gloves and place the baking sheets on the chopping board. Switch off the oven.

12. Use the palette knife to lift the biscuits onto the cooling rack.

biscuits, cakes and sweets

Sugar biscuits

Take out

2 baking sheets, measuring cups
measuring spoons, sieve
large mixing bowl
pastry blender, whisk
small mixing bowl
fork, teaspoon, oven gloves
chopping board
palette knife (spatula) or egg lifter
cooling rack

What you'll need

250 ml self-raising flour
50 ml cornflour (Maizena®)
60 ml castor sugar
1 ml salt
60 ml butter or margarine
1 egg
2 ml vanilla essence

1. Set the oven temperature to 180 °C (350 °F).

2. Grease the baking sheets with butter or margarine.

3. Sift the self-raising flour, cornflour, castor sugar and salt together in the large mixing bowl.

4. Add the butter or margarine and rub it into the flour mixture with your fingertips or cut it in with the pastry blender. It should look like fine breadcrumbs.

5. Whisk the egg and vanilla essence together in the small mixing bowl. Add this to the flour mixture and mix with a fork.

6. Knead the dough until it is smooth.

7. Break off 24 pieces of dough with a teaspoon. Roll them into balls with your hands.

The dough can also be formed into figures, animals and different shapes. (see the picture on p. 144).

8. Arrange the balls or figures about 8 cm apart on the baking sheets. Flatten each ball with a teaspoon.

9. Bake one sheet at a time for 15 minutes. Remove the sheets from the oven using the oven gloves and place them on the chopping board. Switch off the oven.

10. Lift the biscuits from the baking sheets with the palette knife. Allow them to cool on the cooling rack.

Suggestions for fancy sugar biscuits.

Butter icing

Take out

measuring cups, sieve
2 mixing bowls, measuring spoons
wooden spoon or
  electric hand mixer
table knife

What you'll need

600 ml icing sugar
100 ml soft butter or margarine
15–30 ml boiling water
5 ml vanilla essence
few drops food colouring (optional)

1. Sift the icing sugar into one mixing bowl.

2. Measure out the butter or margarine into the other mixing bowl.

3. Beat the butter or margarine with the wooden spoon or electric hand mixer. Gradually add 500 ml icing sugar.

4. Add 15 ml boiling water and the vanilla essence and beat. Add the remaining icing sugar and beat again until the icing is light and creamy. Add another 5 ml boiling water if the icing is too thick to spread.

5. Add the colouring and mix very well. Spread the butter icing on the cake or fairy cakes with a table knife.

biscuits, cakes and sweets

Take out

pencil
round cake tin,
   22 cm in diameter
baking paper, scissors
measuring cups, 2 mixing bowls
wooden spoon or
   electric hand mixer
tablespoon, measuring spoons
sieve, measuring jug
plastic scraper
oven gloves, chopping board
table knife, cooling rack

What you'll need

125 g soft butter or margarine
250 ml castor sugar
5 ml vanilla essence
2 eggs
500 ml cake flour
15 ml baking powder
2 ml salt
150 ml lukewarm milk
butter icing (p. 145)
colourful sweets to decorate

Party cake
(butter cake)

1. Set the oven temperature to 180 °C (350 °F).

2. Trace the cake tin on the baking paper and cut out the circle. Line the cake tin with the paper circle and grease with butter or margarine.

3. Follow the instructions for fairy cakes (cupcakes) **(p. 137)** from step **3** to step **8**.

4. Turn the batter into the greased cake tin. Scrape all the batter from the mixing bowl with the plastic scraper. Spread evenly on top.

5. Bake the cake for 25 minutes. When the cake is done, it will shrink away from the sides of the tin. Remove it from the oven with oven gloves and place it on the chopping board. Switch off the oven.

6. Run the knife along the sides of the cake to loosen it from the tin. Turn it out onto the cooling rack. Remove the paper and leave it to cool completely.

7. Spread the cake with butter icing, using a knife. Decorate it with the sweets.

A small plastic bag can be used as an icing tube. Cut a small piece from one corner.

Take out

tart dish, 22 cm in diameter
measuring cups
measuring spoons, sieve
large mixing bowl
measuring jug, small saucepan
small mixing bowl, whisk
wooden spoon, plastic scraper
oven gloves
cooling rack

What you'll need

250 ml cake flour
125 ml castor sugar
20 ml baking powder
1 ml salt
125 ml milk
50 ml butter or margarine
1 egg
50 ml honey
25 ml butter

Honey cake

1. Set the oven temperature to 180 °C (350 °F).

2. Grease the tart dish with butter or margarine.

3. Sift the flour, sugar, baking powder and salt together into the large mixing bowl.

4. Pour the milk into the saucepan and add the 50 ml butter or margarine. Put the saucepan on the stove plate and switch the heat to medium. Remove the saucepan from the heat as soon as the butter or margarine has melted and switch off the stove plate.

5. Beat the egg in the small mixing bowl with the whisk. Stir it into the milk mixture with the wooden spoon.

6. Stir the lukewarm milk mixture rapidly into the flour mixture until it is smooth. Do not let it stand.

biscuits, cakes and sweets

7. Turn the batter immediately into the tart dish. Scrape the mixing bowl with the plastic scraper.

8. Bake it immediately for 15 minutes.

9. While the cake is in the oven, clean the saucepan. Measure out the honey and butter into the saucepan.

10. Turn the stove plate to low heat. Melt the honey and butter. Do not let it boil. Switch off the heat.

11. Remove the honey cake from the oven with oven gloves and place it on the cooling rack. Switch off the oven.

12. Pour the melted honey and butter mixture over the entire surface of the cake while it is still hot.

Peanut clusters

15 CLUSTERS

Take out

baking sheet, small double boiler
silicone or wooden spoon, fork
2 teaspoons

What you'll need

100 g milk chocolate
100 g unsalted peanuts

1. Grease the baking sheet with butter or margarine. Switch on a stove plate to medium heat.

2. Pour 500 ml hot water into the bottom half of the double boiler. Put it on the hot stove plate.

3. Break the chocolate into the top of the double boiler.

4. Slowly melt the chocolate over the hot water. Remove the top half of the double boiler immediately when the chocolate has melted.

5. Stir the peanuts into the chocolate with the fork. Mix well.

6. Use 2 teaspoons to drop peanut clusters onto the greased baking sheet. Work rapidly while the chocolate is still hot. Leave them to cool.

biscuits, cakes and sweets

Take out

baking sheets
measuring cups
measuring jug, saucepan
wooden or silicone spoon
chopping board
measuring spoons
2 teaspoons

What you'll need

125 g butter or margarine
500 ml sugar
125 ml cocoa
125 ml milk
750 ml oats
250 ml desiccated coconut
5 ml vanilla essence

Chocolate clusters

1. Grease the baking sheets with butter or margarine.

2. Measure out the butter, sugar, cocoa and milk and empty into the saucepan.

3. Switch on the stove plate to medium and cook the mixture in the saucepan, stirring with a wooden or silicone spoon until it starts boiling.

4. Immediately turn the heat to low and let the mixture boil for exactly 5 minutes. Take the saucepan off the stove plate and put it on the chopping board. Switch off the heat.

5. Add the oats, coconut and vanilla essence and mix well.

6. Spoon small lumps of the mixture onto the baking sheets with 2 teaspoons while the mixture is hot.

7. Leave to cool until firm.

biscuits, cakes and sweets

FUDGE

Take out

flat dish or pan
 (20 cm x 30 cm)
measuring cups
measuring spoons
measuring jug, saucepan
wooden spoon
chopping board, plastic scraper
table knife, serving plate

What you'll need

750 ml sugar
1 ml salt
250 ml cream
250 ml desiccated coconut
5 ml vanilla essence
butter or margarine

Coconut fudge

1. Grease the dish or pan with butter or margarine.

2. Measure out the sugar, salt and cream into the saucepan.

3. Switch on the stove plate to medium. Place the saucepan on the heat and stir the mixture with the wooden spoon until the sugar has dissolved.

4. Add the coconut to the sugar mixture. Let it boil for 10 minutes. Stir occasionally with the wooden spoon. Switch off the heat.

5. Remove the saucepan from the stove and put it on the chopping board. Stir in the vanilla essence.

6. Stir the fudge with the wooden spoon until it starts to thicken. When it starts to thicken, stop stirring.

7. Scrape the fudge into the greased pan with the plastic scraper and level on top.

8. Cut the coconut fudge into squares and leave to cool completely. Lift them onto the serving plate with the knife.

biscuits, cakes and sweets

Crispies

35 SQUARES

Take out

flat dish or pan
   (40 cm x 25 cm)
measuring cups
mixing bowl, measuring jug
double boiler
wooden or silicone spoon
measuring spoons
palette knife (spatula)
table knife, serving dish

What you'll need

1,5 litres rice crispies
125 ml chopped pecan nuts
60 ml butter or margarine
250 g marshmallows
2 ml vanilla essence

1. Grease the flat dish or pan with butter or margarine.

2. Measure out the rice crispies and nuts into the mixing bowl.

3. Pour 750 ml hot water into the bottom half of the double boiler. Put it on the stove and switch on the heat to medium. Leave it to boil.

4. Measure out the butter or margarine into the top of the double boiler and put it over the hot water.

5. Add the marshmallows to the butter in the top part of the double boiler. Stir until it has melted. Add the vanilla essence and stir.

6. Pour the hot marshmallow mixture over the rice crispies in the mixing bowl. Switch off the heat. Stir until the rice crispies and nuts cling together.

7. Press the mixture into the greased pan with the palette knife.

8. Leave it to cool and cut it into squares. Use the palette knife to lift out the crispies onto the serving dish.

biscuits, cakes and sweets 157

Nut caramels

Take out

flat dish or oven pan
   (20 cm x 20 cm)
measuring cups
sieve, mixing bowl, saucepan
wooden spoon, chopping board
measuring spoons, plastic scraper
tablespoon
table knife

What you'll need

500 ml icing sugar
125 ml butter or margarine
250 ml brown sugar
60 ml milk
250 ml broken walnuts
   or pecan nuts
5 ml vanilla essence

1. Grease the dish or oven pan with butter or margarine.

2. Sift the icing sugar into the mixing bowl.

3. Measure out the butter or margarine and brown sugar into the saucepan.

4. Switch on the stove plate to medium heat and put the saucepan on it.

5. Stir all the time with the wooden spoon while the butter or margarine and sugar melt together. Let it boil for 2 minutes. Stir continuously.

6. Add the milk a little at a time, stirring well after every addition. Be careful that it does not splash. Keep on stirring until it boils again. Switch off the heat.

7. Remove the saucepan from the stove and put it on the chopping board. Leave it to cool until it is lukewarm.

8. Beat a little icing sugar at a time into the caramel mixture, using the wooden spoon.

9. Add the nuts and vanilla essence. Stir until it thickens.

10. Scrape the mixture into the greased pan and level the top with the tablespoon.

11. Put it in the fridge to cool. Cut the nut caramel into squares.

biscuits, cakes and sweets **159**

who did the cooking?

Teresa Steyn

Age:
9

Which is your favourite recipe?
Pizza.

What do you like best about cooking?
I like making waffles at home and the best part is when I get to lick the bowl of batter clean!

Mikhe Botha

Age:
10

Which is your favourite recipe?
I loved the chocolate clusters and kept going back for more.

What do you like best about cooking?
Having to taste all the time to see if I am getting it right.

Luam Staples

Age:
9

Which is your favourite recipe?
Date surprises.

What do you like best about cooking?
I enjoyed the excitement of it all and the tasting. Cooking is fun!

Inge Meyer

Age:
6

Which is your favourite recipe?
The sugar biscuits are my favourite, but I also enjoyed tasting all the other biscuit doughs.

What do you like best about cooking?
I like to lick out the mixing bowl and to roll biscuit dough into a ball and then let it melt in my mouth.

Chandler Jafta

Age:
11

Which is your favourite recipe?
Crispies.

What do you like best about cooking?
I like to experiment and try out new recipes.

Elsa-Marié van der Watt

Age:
7

Which is your favourite recipe?
Pancakes.

What do you like best about cooking?
I love spending time in the kitchen with my mom.

Braam van der Vyver

Age:
8

Which is your favourite recipe?
I liked the orange pudding best because I love pudding!

What do you like best about cooking?
Cutting out scones was fun.

Ilse de Lange

Age:
8

Which is your favourite recipe?
Chocolate milkshake.

What do you like best about cooking?
Licking out the mixing bowl after making a chocolate cake or icing!

Daniël Wiese

Age:
8

Which is your favourite recipe?
I'm still dreaming about the milkshake I made. It was so much fun to make and share with Ilse.

What do you like best about cooking?
The best part is licking the spoons and mixing bowls clean, even though my mom thinks it's disgusting!

index

A

Apple and yoghurt breakfast	34
Apple Brown Betty	106
Apple crumble (see Brown Betty)	

B

Bake	19
Baked meatballs	66
Baked potatoes	88
Baked sago pudding	104
Baking sheet	14
Banana smoothie	26
Beans, boiled green	84
Biscuits, orange	140
Biscuits, peanut butter	132
Biscuits, sugar	142
Blender, pastry	14
Board, chopping	14
Boil	19
Boiled eggs	36
Boiled green beans	84
Boiled potatoes	86
Boiled rice	83
Bolognaise sauce	68
Bran muffins	116
Break, an egg	19
Breakfast, apple and yoghurt	34
Breakfast scones	110
Brown Betty, apple	106
Brush, pastry	16
Brush, vegetable	15
Butter	13
Butter cake	146
Butter icing	145

C

Cake, honey	148
Cake, party	146
Cakes, fish	62
Cakes, fairy	137
Caramels, nut	158
Carbohydrates	10
Carrots, to prepare for salad	80
Casserole, chicken	58
Casserole, tuna	60
Cereals	10
Cheese, scrambled eggs and	38
Cheese, scones	114
Cheese, toasted	42
Chicken à la king	54

Chicken casserole	58
Chicken, crumbed breasts	56
Chips, oven	90
Chocolate clusters	152
Chocolate milkshake	27
Chop	19
Chopping board	14
Clusters, chocolate	152
Clusters, peanut	151
Coconut fudge	154
Colander	16
Cookies, oats and raisins	130
Cooling rack	17
Cream	19
Crisp custard squares	134
Crispies	156
Crisp salad, packed	78
Crumbed chicken breasts	56
Crumpets	118
Crush	20
Cucumber, to prepare for salad	81
Cupcakes	137
Cups, measuring	12
Custard	98
Custard, crisp squares	134
Cut in	20
Cut in wedges	20

D

Dainty sandwiches	124
Date surprises	128
Dissolve	20
Double boiler	17
Drain	20
Drink, iced party	28
Drinks	24

E

Egg lifter	17
Egg, to break	19
Egg, to separate	22
Eggs, boiled	36
Eggs, scrambled	38
Electric hand mixer	16
Equipment, kitchen	14

F

Facts about foods	10
Fairy cakes	137
Fish	10

Fish cakes	62
Flake	20
Fold in	21
Food processor	17
Foods, facts about	10
French toast	40
Fruit, in the diet	11
Fry	21
Frying pan	14
Fudge, coconut	154

G

Grate	21
Grater	15
Grease	21
Green beans, boiled	84
Green salad, tossed	76

H

Hamburgers	48
Honey cake	148
Hot dogs	46

I

Iced party drink	28
Icing, butter	145

J

Jelly	97

K

Kitchen equipment	14
Kitchen scissors	15
Kitchen tongs	15
Knead	21
Knife, palette	15
Knife, table	14
Knife, vegetable	15

L

Lettuce, to wash	79

M

Macaroni cheese	50
Margarine	13
Measure	12
Measuring cups	12
Measuring spoons	12

Meat	10
Meatballs, baked	66
Melt	21
Milkshake, chocolate	27
Mince, savoury	68
Minerals, in the diet	10, 11
Mix	22
Muffin pan	14
Muffins, bran	116

N

Noodles	10
Nut caramels	158

O

Oats and raisin cookies	130
Oats porridge in the microwave	35
Orange biscuits	140
Orange pudding	100
Oven chips	90
Oven gloves	8
Oven temperatures	17

P

Packed crisp salad	78
Palette knife (spatula)	15
Pancakes	120
Pan, frying	14
Pan, muffin	14
Party cake	146
Party drink, iced	28
Pastry blender	14
Pastry brush	16
Peanut butter biscuits	132
Peanut clusters	151
Peeler, vegetable	15
Peppers, sweet, to prepare for salad	80
Pinch, of salt	13
Pineapple, to prepare for salad	82
Pizza	70
Plastic scraper	15
Porridge, oats in the microwave	35
Potatoes, baked	88
Potatoes, boiled	86
Potholders	8
Processor, food	17
Proteins	10

Pudding, baked sago	104
Pudding, orange	100

R

Raisin and oats cookies	130
Rice, boiled	83
Rub in	22

S

Sago, baked pudding	104
Salad, packed crisp	78
Salad ingredients	79
Salad, tossed green	76
Salt, a pinch of	13
Sandwiches, dainty	124
Sauce, bolognaise	68
Sauce, white	53
Sauté	22
Savoury mince	68
Scissors, kitchen	15
Scones, breakfast	110
Scones, cheese	114
Scrambled eggs and cheese	38
Separate an egg	22
Sheet, baking	14

Shred	22
Simmer	22
Slice	23
Smoothie, banana	26
Spatula	15
Spoons, measuring	12
Spoon, wooden	15
Squares, crisp custard	134
Stew	23
Stir	23
Stir-fry	23
Sugar	11
Sugar biscuits	142
Surprises, date	128
Sweet pepper, to prepare for salad	80
Sweets	11

T

Table knife	14
Tea for two	30
Toast, French	40
Toasted cheese	42
Tomatoes, to prepare for salad	81
Tongs, kitchen	15
Tossed green salad	76

Trifle	95
Tuna casserole	60

U

Utensils	14

V

Vegetable brush	15
Vegetable knife	15
Vegetable peeler	15
Vegetables	11
Vegetables, boiled	84
Vitamins	10, 11
Volume	13

W

Wash up	9
Weight	12
Whip	23
Whisk	23
White sauce	53
Widths	13
Wooden spoon	15
Words to know	19

Y

Yoghurt, and apple breakfast	34

index 171